GETTING TO KNOW THE WORLD'S GREATEST ARTISTS

G R A N D M A
MOSES

WRITTEN AND ILLUSTRATED BY MIKE VENEZIA

CHILDREN'S PRESS®
A DIVISION OF SCHOLASTIC INC.
NEW YORK TORONTO LONDON AUCKLAND SYDNEY
MEXICO CITY NEW DELHI HONG KONG
DANBURY, CONNECTICUT

For Kiki—my most animated friend!

Cover: *Sugaring Off,* by Grandma Moses. 1943, oil on pressed wood, 23 x 27 in.
© Grandma Moses Properties Co., New York/Private Collection, courtesy of Galerie St. Etienne, New York.

Colorist for illustrations: Dave Ludwig

Library of Congress Cataloging-in-Publication Data

Venezia, Mike.
  Grandma Moses / written and illustrated by Mike Venezia.
     p. cm. — (Getting to know the world's greatest artists)
  Summary: An introduction to the life and work of the twentieth-century
American painter known as Grandma Moses.
  ISBN 0-516-22027-6 (lib. bdg.)   0-516-27913-0 (pbk.)
  1. Moses, Grandma, 1860-1961—Juvenile literature. 2.
Painters—United States—Biography—Juvenile literature. [1. Moses,
Grandma, 1860-1961. 2. Artists. 3. Women—Biography. 4. Painting,
American.] I. Title. II. Series. Venezia, Mike. Getting to know the
world's greatest artists.
  ND237.M78 V46 2003
  759.13—dc21

                               2002015129

1 2 3 4 5 6 7 8 9 10 R 12 11 10 09 08 07 06 05 04 03

Grandma Moses at Work, 1946. © Grandma Moses Properties Co., New York, photograph by Otto Kallir.

Anna Mary "Grandma" Moses was born in 1860 on a farm in Greenwich, New York. Grandma Moses didn't start to paint seriously until she was almost 70 years old. At first, no one paid much attention to her pictures. But by the time she died at the age of 101, Grandma Moses had become one of America's most famous and best-loved artists.

Joy Ride, by Grandma Moses. 1953, oil on pressed wood, 18 x 24 in. © Grandma Moses Properties Co., New York/Private Collection, courtesy of Galerie St. Etienne, New York.

Grandma Moses never thought her pictures were anything special. She started to paint for fun and to help pass the time. When she was 92 years old, a book about her life was published. Grandma Moses hardly mentioned

Apple Butter Making, by Grandma Moses. 1947, oil on pressed wood, 16 1/2 x 23 5/8 in.
© Grandma Moses Properties Co., New York/Private Collection.

her artwork in the book. Instead she told about the adventures she had growing up on her farm. Many of Grandma Moses's paintings are scenes of her favorite memories.

Just about all of Grandma Moses's paintings are landscapes. They show the beautiful rolling mountains, towns, and farms where she lived. Unlike most landscape painters, though, Grandma Moses included people doing all kinds of interesting things, like making tasty apple butter or candles, or celebrating a favorite holiday or season of the year.

For This is the Fall of the Year, by Grandma Moses. 1947, oil on pressed wood, 16 x 21 3/4 in.
© Grandma Moses Properties Co., New York/Private Collection.

The type of artwork Grandma Moses created is called folk art. Folk art is made by artists who haven't had art classes or any special art training. Folk artists usually learn to draw, paint, or make sculptures all on their own. Sometimes Grandma Moses learned by copying from old prints, calendars, and greeting cards.

Checkered House, by Grandma Moses. 1943, oil on pressed wood, 36 x 45 in.
© Grandma Moses Properties Co., New York/IBM Corporation, Armonk, New York.

Detail showing animals and figures from *Peaceable Kingdom,* by Edward Hicks. c. 1834, oil on canvas, 29 3/8 x 35 1/2 in. © Corbis Images/Burstein Collection.

Tiger, by Morris Hirshfield. 1940, oil on canvas, 28 x 39 7/8 in. © Robert and Gail Rentzer for Estate of Morris Hirshfield/Licensed by VAGA, New York, NY. Photo © Art Resource, NY/Scala/The Museum of Modern Art, New York, Abby Aldrich Rockefeller Fund (00328.1941)

Grandma Moses and other folk artists, like Edward Hicks and Morris Hirshfield, have created some of the most original and interesting works of art ever.

In the 1860s, when Anna Mary Robertson was growing up, kids didn't have televisions, compact-disc players, video games, movies, or shopping malls. There were still plenty of fun things to do, though. Anna Mary and her brothers used their imaginations to make up adventure games.

They played in the forests and hills near
their home. They went ice-skating on the many
ponds surrounding their family farm. They
spent hours sledding down snowy hills, using
shovels, wooden washtubs, and anything else
that would work as a sled. Grandma Moses
said these were the happiest times of her life.

Anna Mary's father sometimes brought home sheets of paper for his children to draw on. Anna Mary loved drawing. Since paint and paintbrushes were too expensive for her family to buy, Anna colored her drawings with berry juice. She dabbed the color on with little sticks or twigs.

Anna Mary said her brothers always made fun of her because she called her finished pictures "lambscapes."

When Anna Mary was 12 years old, she got a job as a housekeeper. Anna helped out families in her area. It was hard work, but she learned a lot about running a home and always found friendly, kind people to work for.

When she was 26 years old, she met a farm worker named Thomas Moses. Thomas and Anna really liked each other. They fell in love and got married about a year later. Thomas and Anna Mary Moses had a long, happy life together. They had lots of children and were very successful farmers.

Washday, by Grandma Moses. 1945, oil on pressed wood, 17 3/4 x 23 1/2 in. © Grandma Moses Properties Co., New York/The Museum of Art, Rhode Island School of Design, Providence, Rhode Island.

One reason Grandma Moses didn't start
painting until she was much older was that as
a young woman, she just didn't have the time.
Aside from doing all her farm duties and
raising a family, Anna Mary started making
butter for a local grocery store.

Then, a few years later, she decided to make potato chips. Anna Mary's butter and potato chips tasted better than anyone else's. Before she knew it, she was busier than ever, making and shipping her products to grocery stores and a nearby resort.

When Grandma Moses was 67 years old, her husband, Thomas, died. Grandma Moses missed him very much. Soon after this happened, she started doing artwork to help pass the time. At first she embroidered, or stitched, scenes out of yarn. She called these works her "worsted pictures." Grandma Moses usually made them as gifts for her friends and relatives.

She continued doing worsted pictures until the knitting and stitching became painful for her fingers. That was when Grandma Moses added painting to her art activities.

The Old Hoosick Bridge, 1818, by Grandma Moses. 1939 or earlier, embroidery yarn on fabric, 10 x 14 in.
© Grandma Moses Properties Co., New York/Private Collection.

Before Grandma Moses could start painting, though, she had to find art supplies. Finding materials for her worsted pictures had never been a problem. Painting supplies, however, were still very expensive and hard to find in rural farm areas.

May: Making Soap, Washing Sheep, by Grandma Moses. 1945, oil on pressed wood, 17 1/4 x 24 1/4 in.
© Grandma Moses Properties Co., New York/Miss Porter's School, Farmington, Connecticut,
Gift of Mrs. Raymond F. Evans.

At first, Grandma Moses used leftover house paint and brushes. She used matchsticks and pins to dab on tiny dots of color. Grandma Moses painted on any surface she could find, including glass windowpanes, sheet metal, and old canvas cloth used to cover farm equipment.

Country Fair, by Grandma Moses. 1950, oil on canvas, 35 x 45 in.
© Grandma Moses Properties Co., New York/Private Collection.

Grandma Moses displayed her artwork at county fairs alongside her canned fruit and jam. One time she won a prize for her jam, but no one even noticed her paintings. Grandma Moses also displayed her paintings in the window of a local drugstore.

Country Fair (detail), by Grandma Moses. 1950, oil on canvas, 35 x 45 in. © Grandma Moses Properties Co., New York/Private Collection.

One day, a man traveling through town stopped by the drugstore. He noticed Grandma Moses's paintings and couldn't believe his eyes. He thought they were wonderful!

Bringing in the Maple Sugar, by Grandma Moses. 1939 or earlier, oil on pressed wood, 14 x 22 in. © Grandma Moses Properties Co., New York/Private Collection, courtesy of Galerie St. Etienne, New York.

Home in Winter, by Grandma Moses. c. 1938, oil on pressed wood, 6 x 16 in. © Grandma Moses Properties Co., New York/Private Collection, courtesy of Galerie St. Etienne, New York.

Louis Caldor was an engineer from New York City. He loved collecting American folk art. Louis bought all the paintings in the drugstore window right away. He then drove to Grandma Moses's house to see if he could buy more of her paintings. Grandma Moses wasn't home at the time, but her daughter-in-law told

Mr. Caldor she thought Grandma Moses had ten more paintings. When Grandma Moses got home, she was excited to hear the good news, but discovered she had only nine paintings. Grandma Moses decided to cut one in half to make ten paintings so Mr. Caldor wouldn't be disappointed when he came back the next day.

Louis Caldor took all of Grandma Moses's paintings back to New York City. He worked as hard as he could to get people interested in displaying and selling them. Unfortunately, it took a long time to get anyone's attention.

River Rouge Plant, by Charles Sheeler. 1932, oil on canvas, 20 x 24 1/8 in.
© Whitney Museum of American Art, New York, Purchase 32.43.

Art dealers in New York didn't really have a problem with Grandma Moses's warm, friendly paintings. Scenes about American life, like those done by such artists as Grant Wood, Edward Hopper, and Charles Sheeler, were pretty popular at the time. It seems there was something else that was a problem for the art dealers.

Louis Caldor found that many art dealers didn't want to take a chance on someone as old as Grandma Moses. They were afraid an artist who was almost 80 years old might become ill and unable to paint any longer. Some dealers felt Grandma Moses might even die soon.

The Quilting Bee, by Grandma Moses. 1950, oil on pressed wood, 20 x 24 in. © Grandma Moses Properties Co., New York/Private Collection, courtesy of Galerie St. Etienne, New York.

Louis Caldor never gave up, and finally found an art dealer who loved Grandma Moses's paintings. This dealer didn't care how old she was, either. Otto Kallir owned the Galerie St. Etienne in New York. He agreed to give Grandma Moses a one-woman show.

Grandma Moses's exhibition helped bring attention to her paintings. Before the show ended, Gimbels, a big department store in New York, asked to use Grandma Moses's paintings for their Thanksgiving festival. Over the next few years, galleries and museums held Grandma Moses exhibitions too. In 1946, a big greeting-card company asked to use some of Grandma Moses's pictures for their collection. Now more people than ever became familiar with her paintings.

Catching the Thanksgiving Turkey, by Grandma Moses. circa 1943, oil on pressed wood, 20 x 24 in.
© Grandma Moses Properties Co., New York/Private Collection, courtesy of Galerie St. Etienne, New York.

People liked Grandma Moses as much as they liked her paintings. She was friendly and fun to talk to. She never let being famous change her life. She always seemed surprised by the amount of money she made from her artwork. By the time Grandma Moses died in 1961, people all over the world knew about her artwork. Grandma Moses's paintings reminded everyone of simpler, happier times.

The works of art in this book came from:

Galerie St. Etienne, New York

The Museum of Art, Rhode Island School of Design, Providence

The Museum of Modern Art, New York

Sheldon Swope Art Museum, Terre Haute

Whitney Museum of American Art, New York